FANCIFUL
FRAME-ABLE
FRACTALS!

(BUTTERFLIES, BUGS AND BIRDS!)

25 UNIQUE, DIGITALLY CREATED FRACTALS SUITABLE FOR FRAMING!

BY: ROSE SANTUCI-SOFRANKO

THIS BOOK IS DEDICATED TO:

OUR LORD:
THE CREATOR OF REAL BUTTERFLIES, BUGS AND BIRDS!

TO MY WONDERFUL HUSBAND, PAUL,
WHO ALWAYS ENCOURAGES ME IN MY ARTWORK!

AND, TO MY SWEET NEPHEW, TOM,
WHO TAUGHT ME HOW TO CREATE
WITH MY IMAGINATION!

(MORE FRACTALS ARE AVAILABLE AT MY ONLINE GALLERY)
http://rose-santucisofranko.artistwebsites.com/art/all/fractals/all

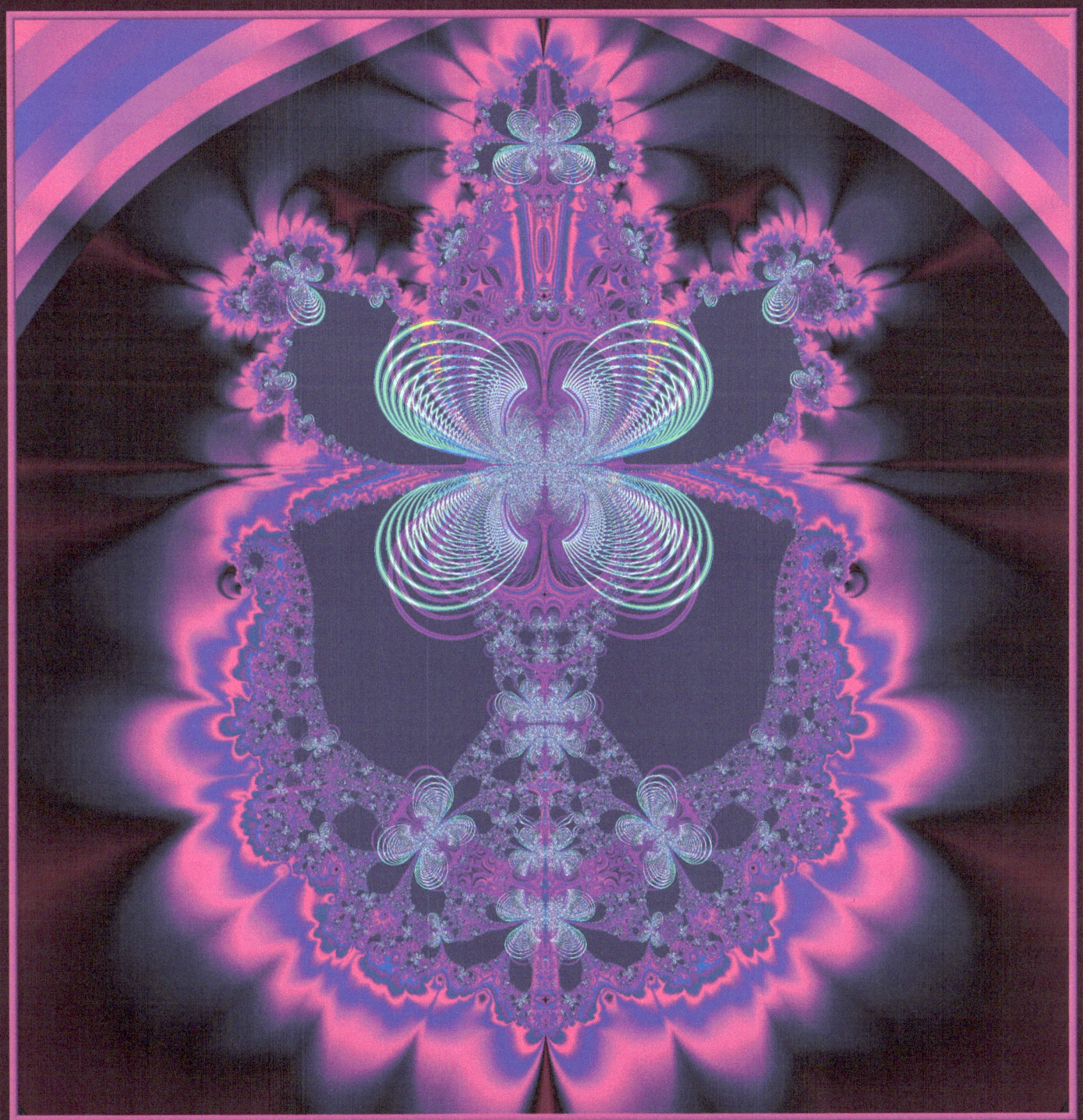

Rose Santuci-Sofranko

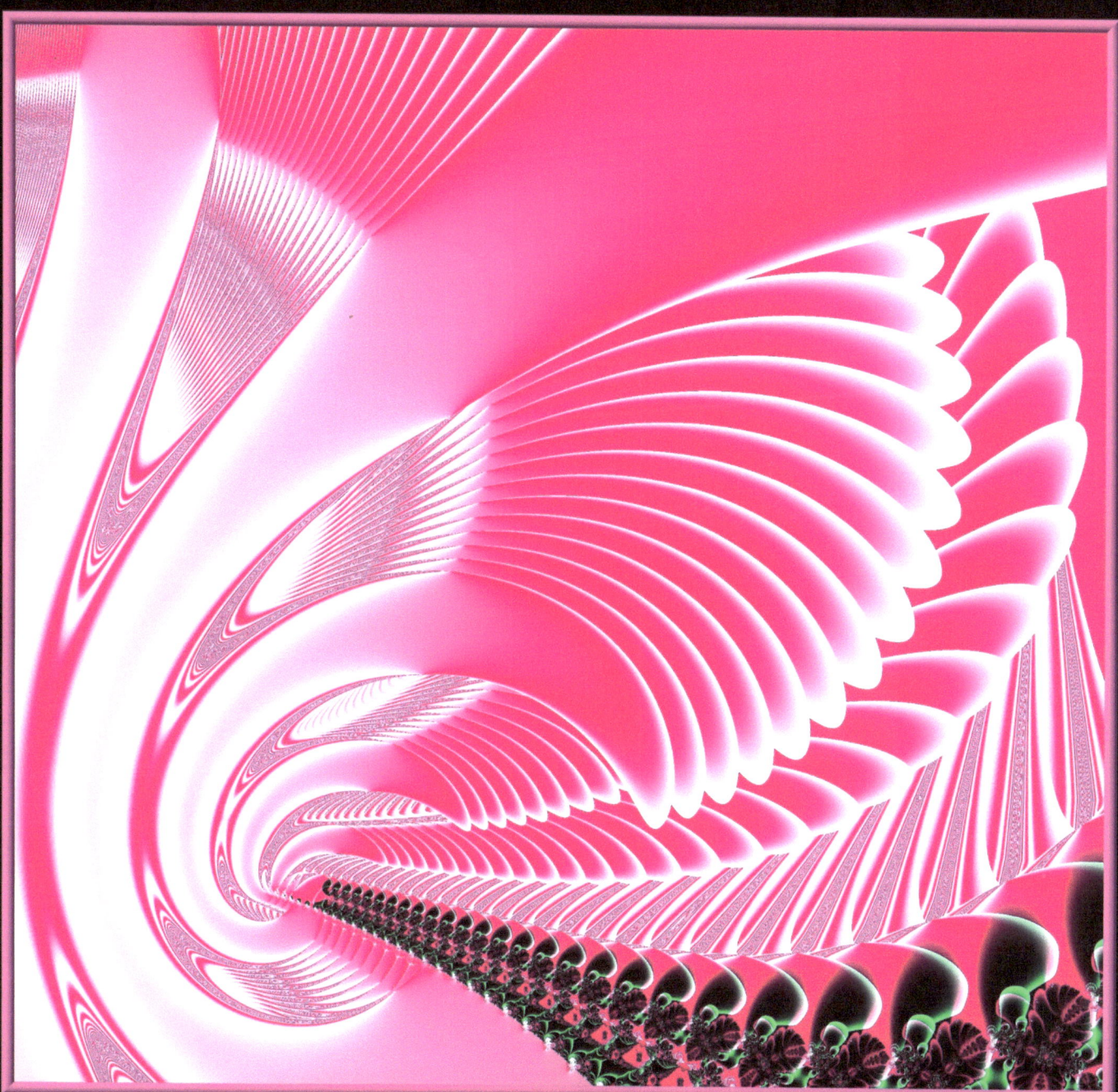

Rose Santuci-Sofranko

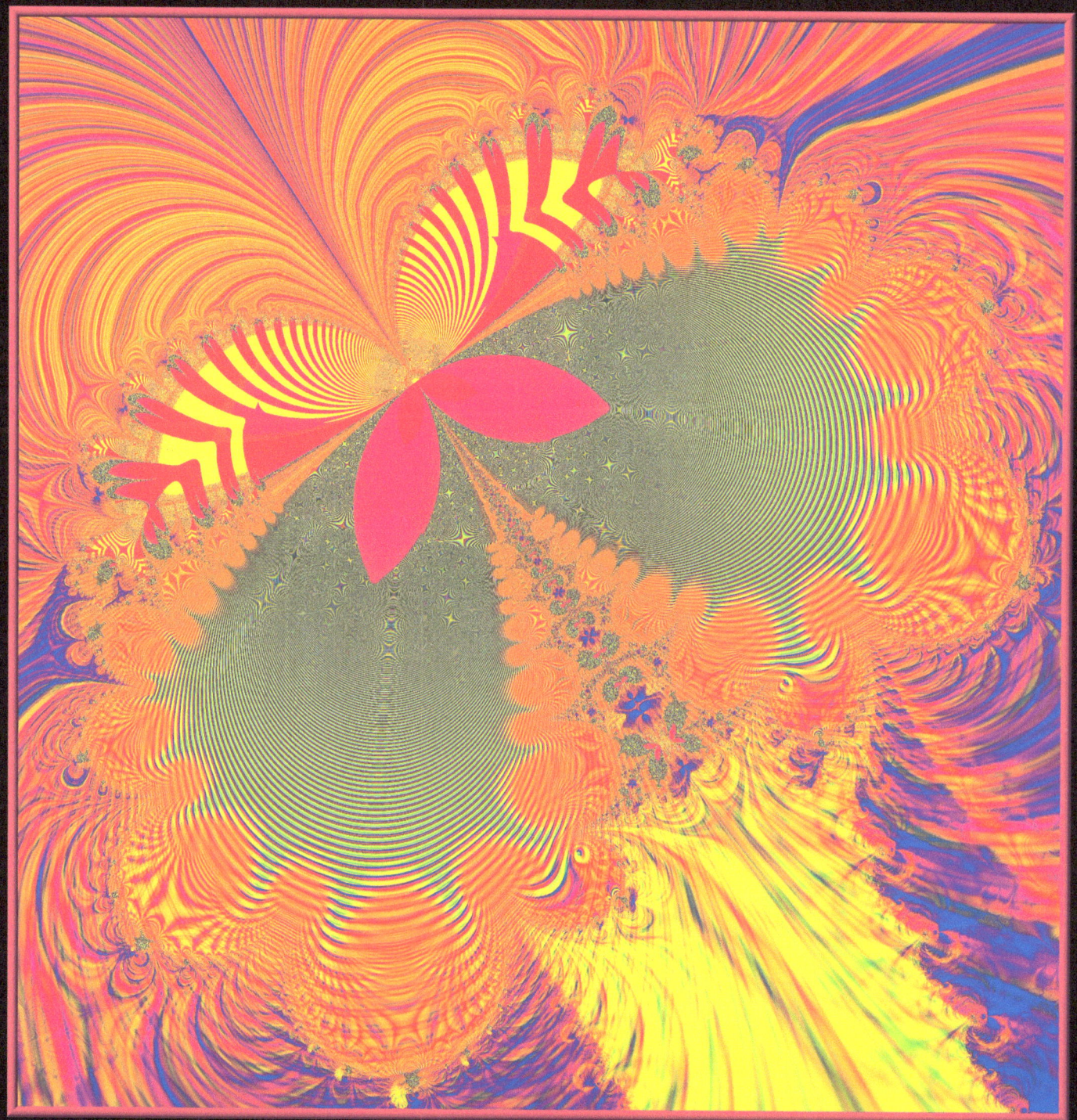

Rose Santuci-Sofranko

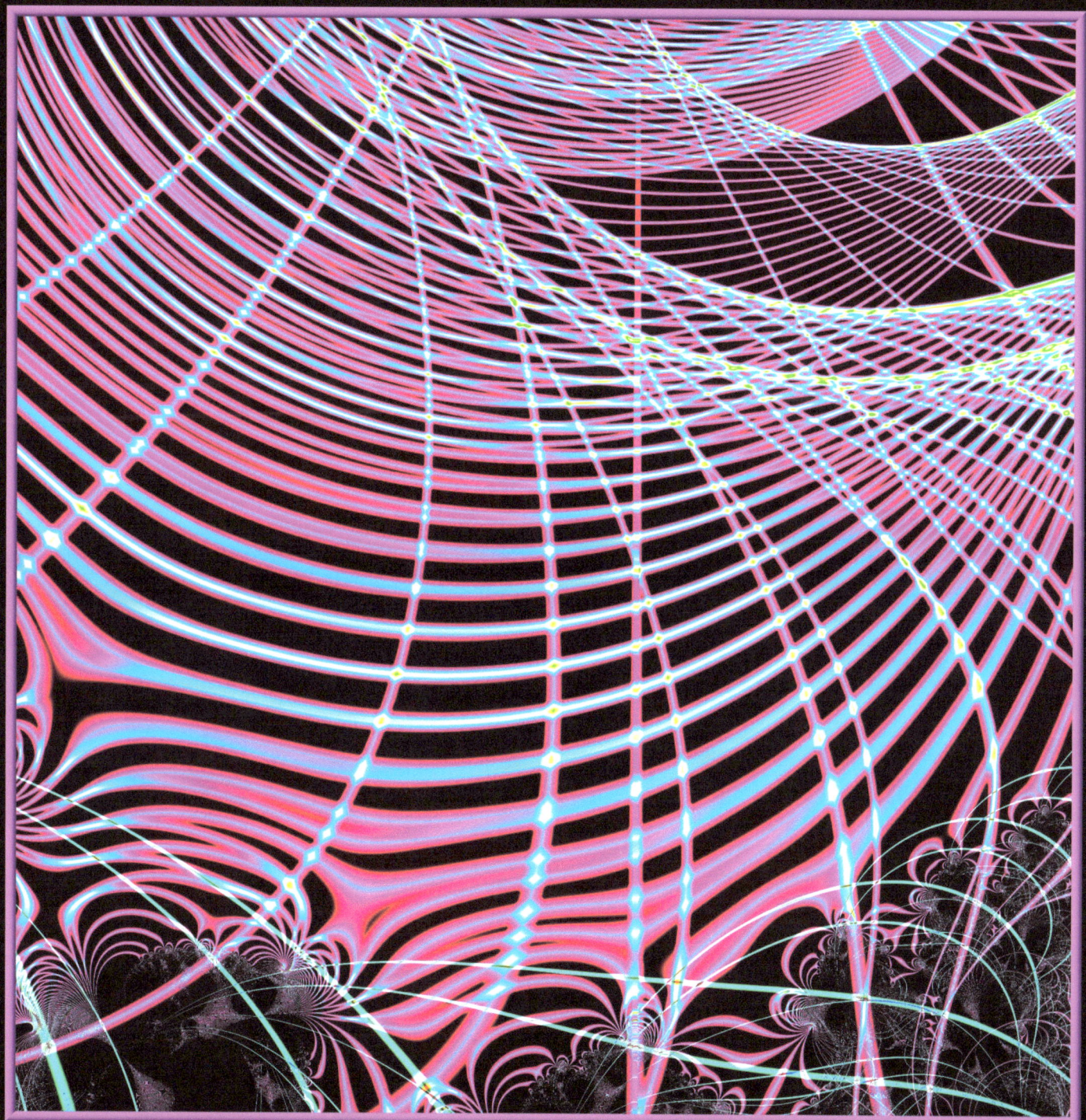

Rose Santuci-Sofranko

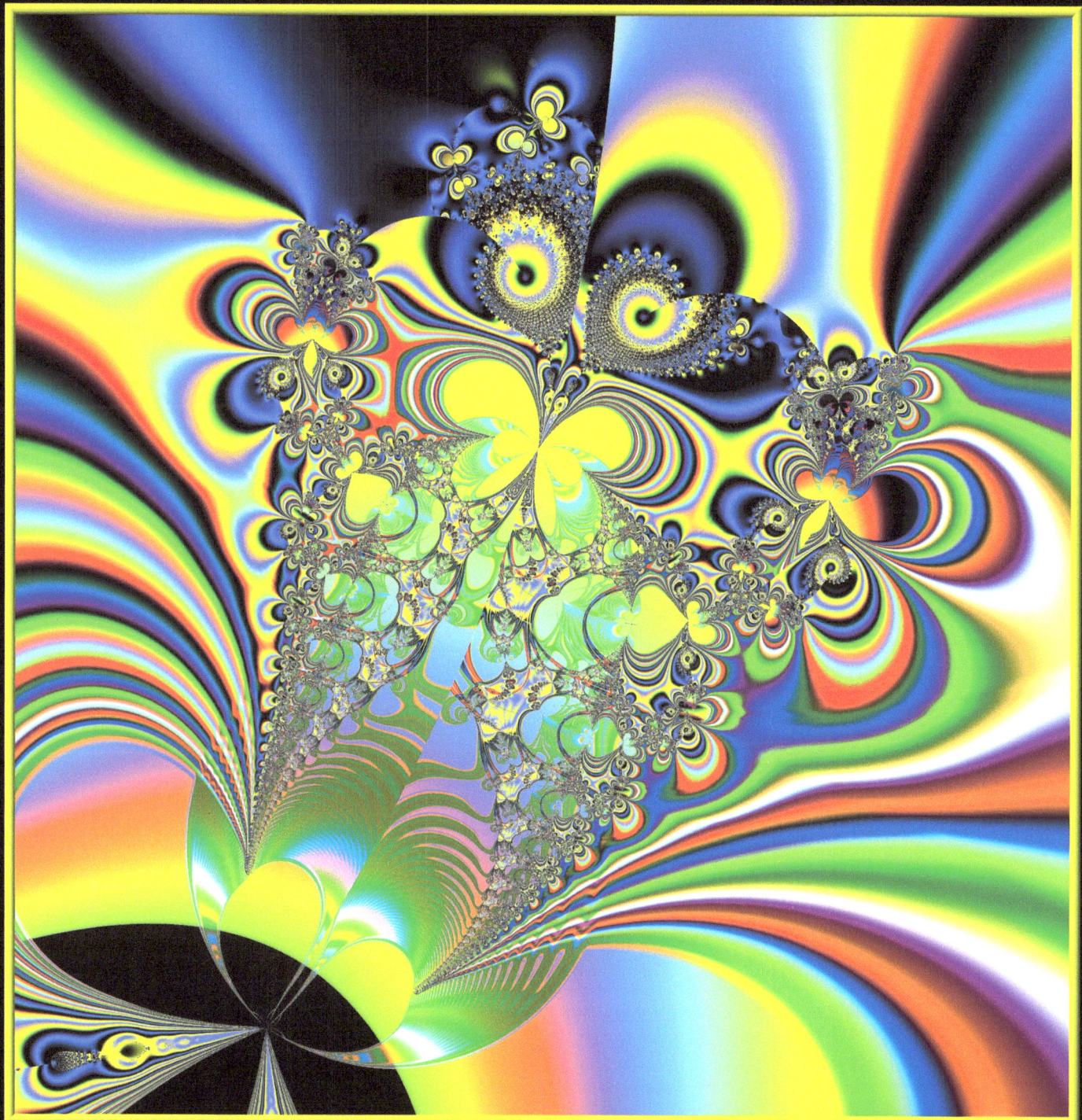
Rose Santuci-Sofranko

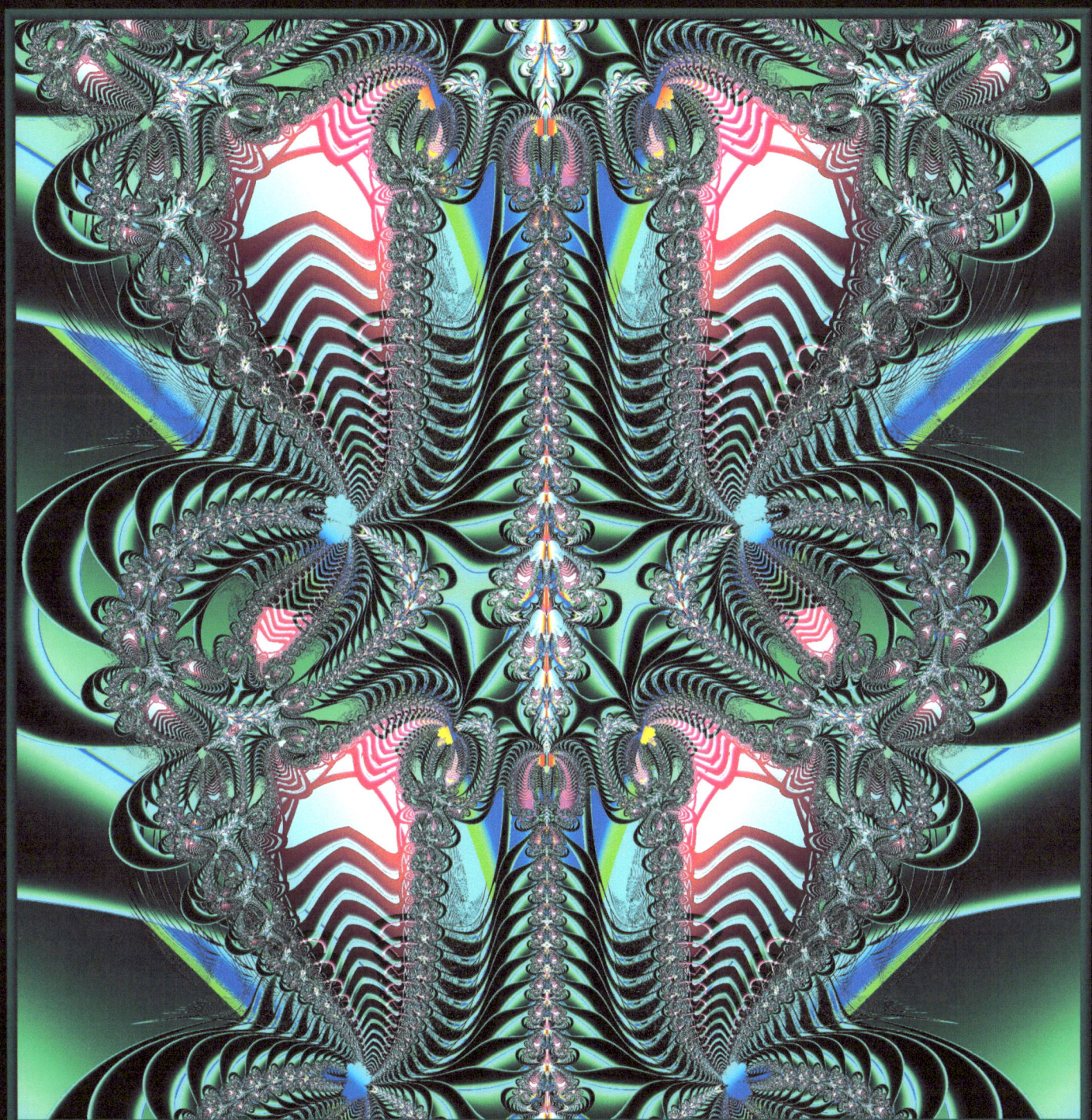

Rose Santuci-Sofranko

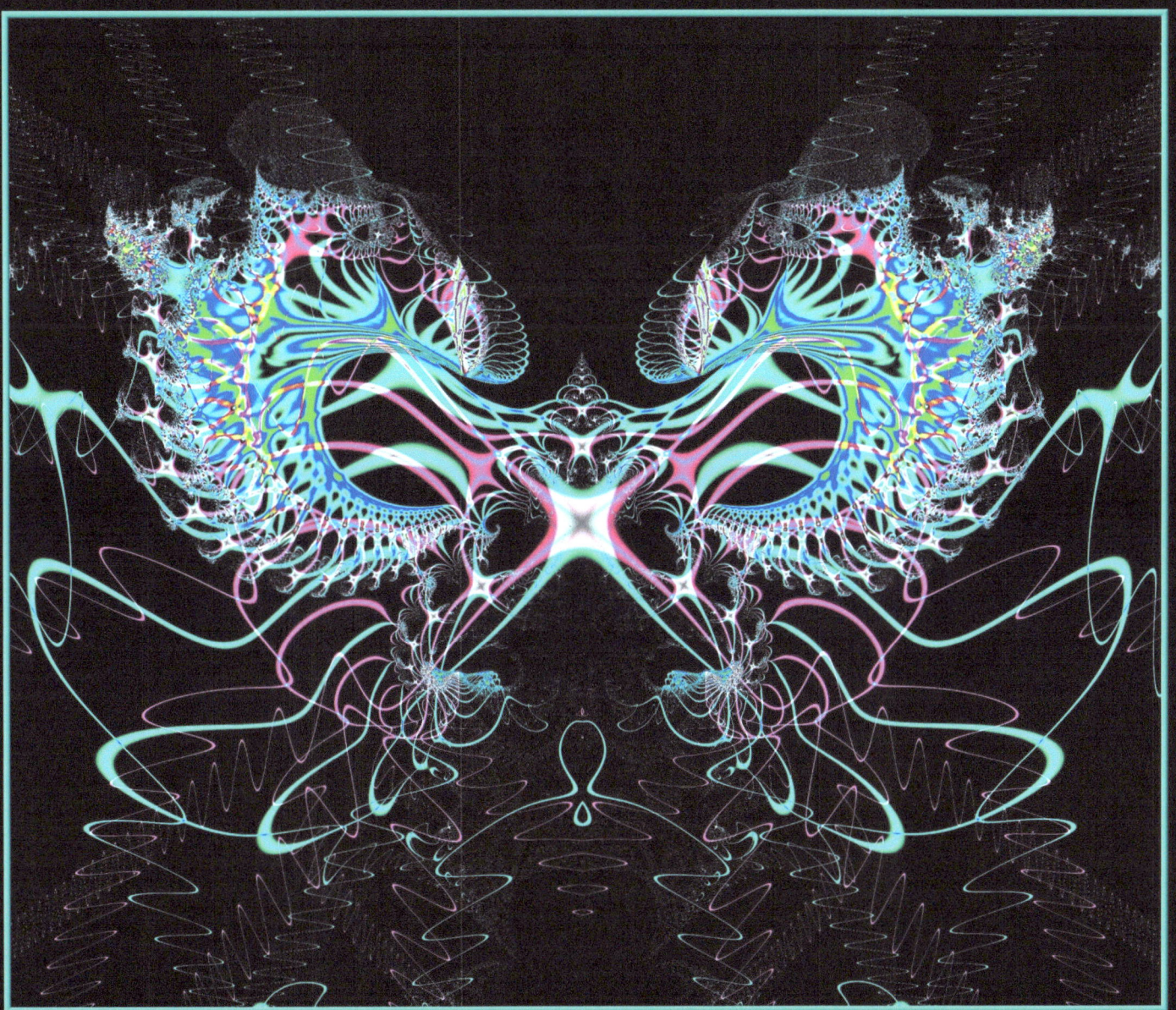
Rose Santuci-Sofranko

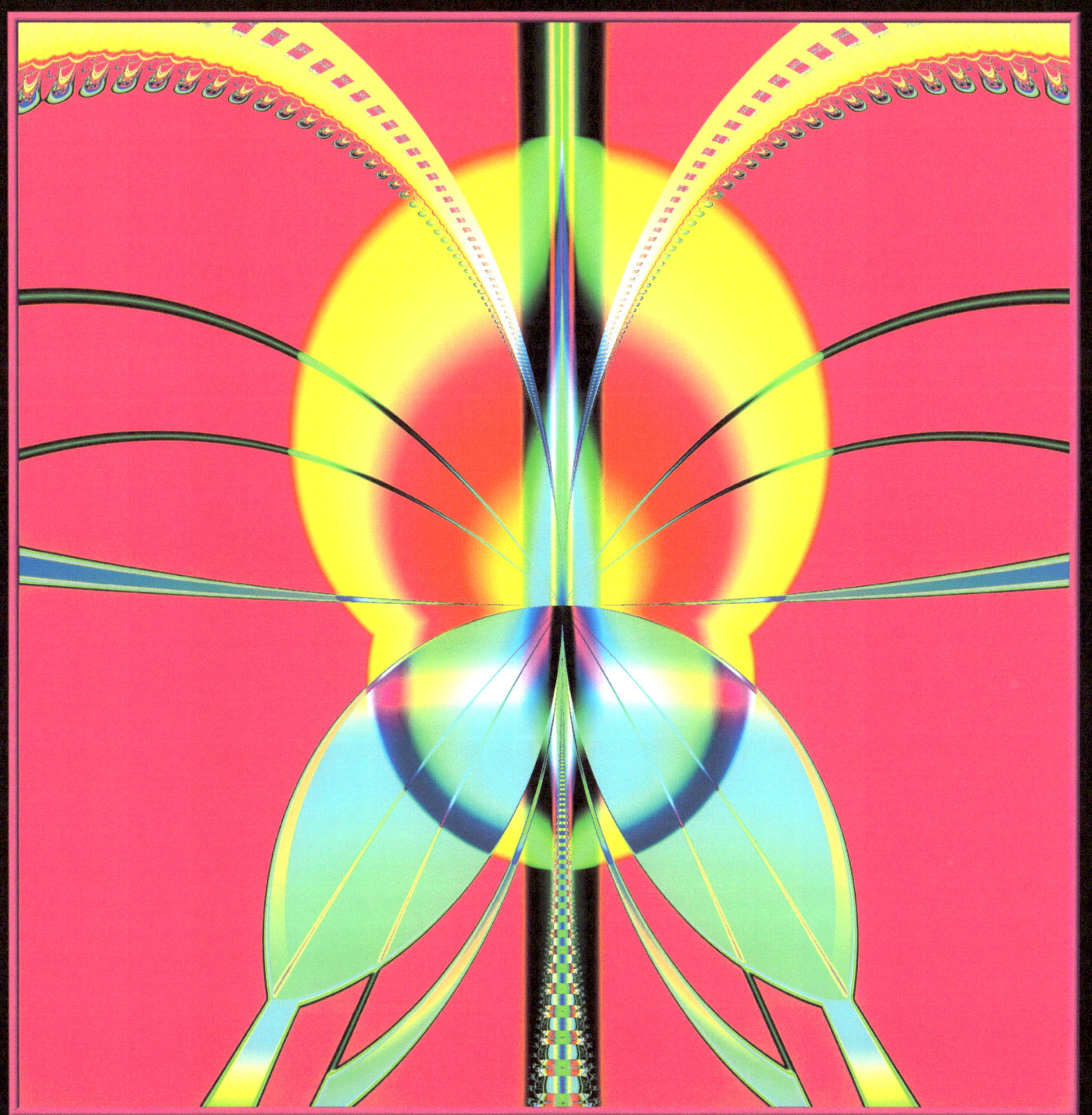

Rose Santuci-Sofranko

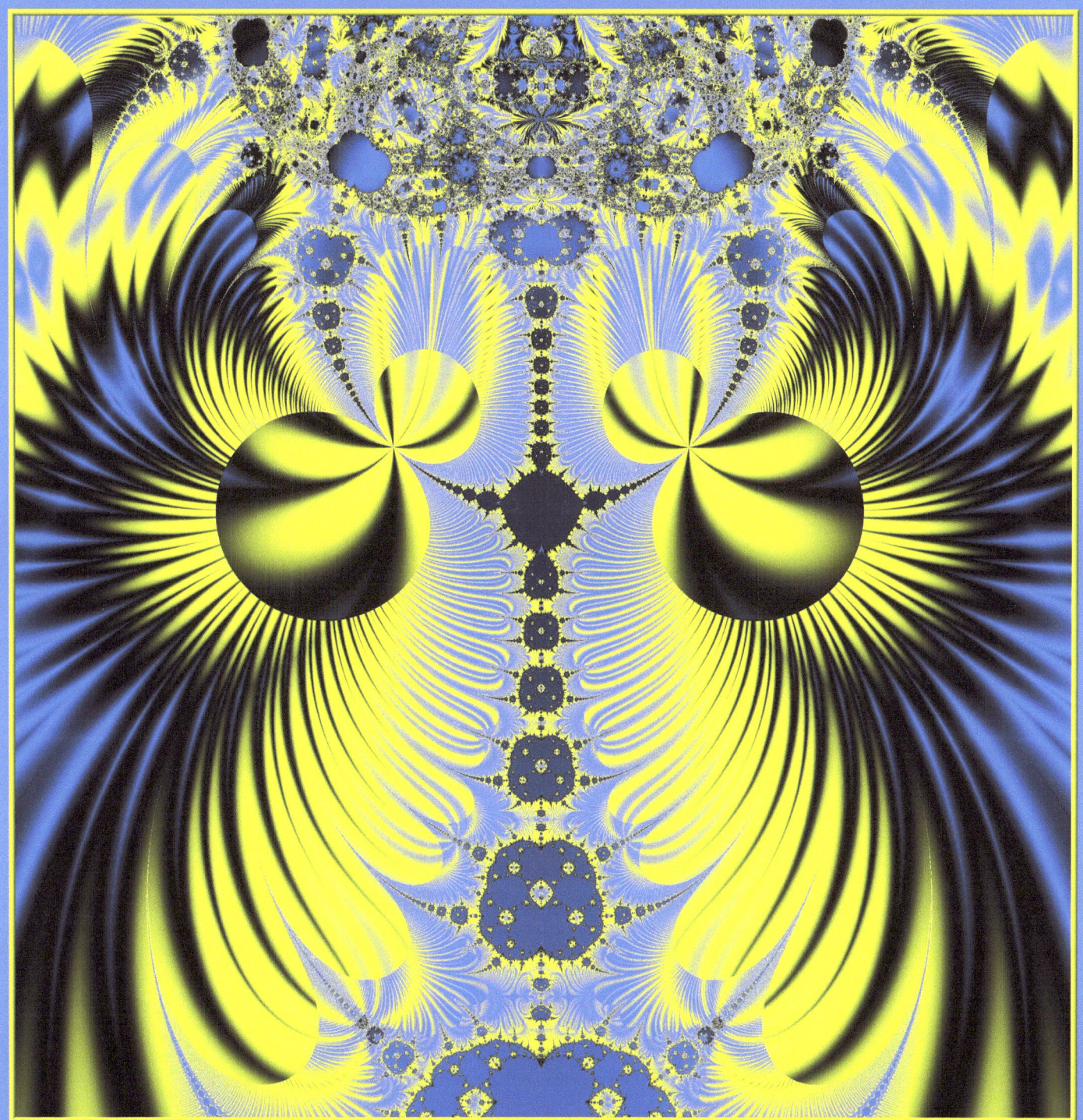

Rose Santuci-Sofranko

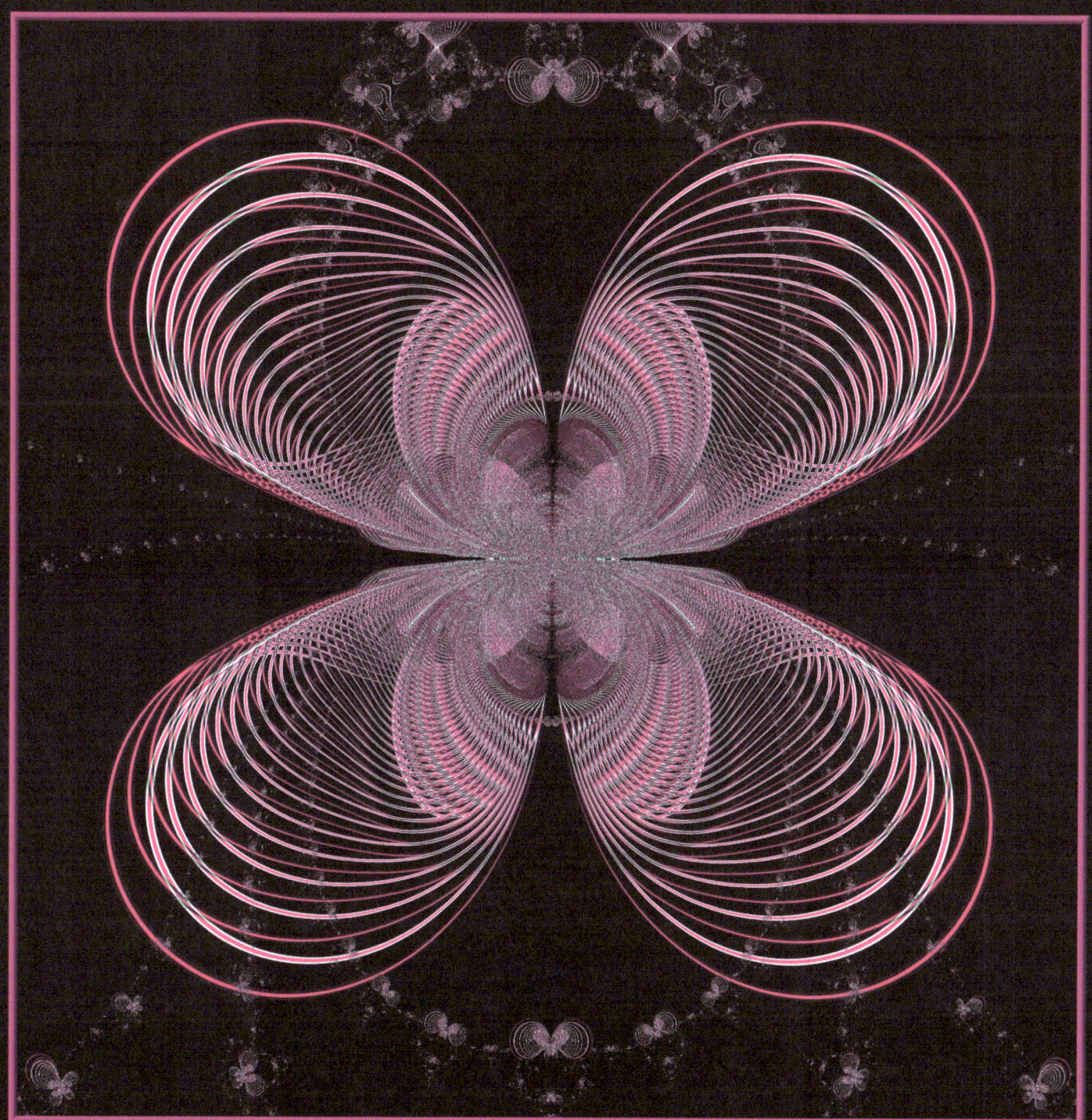

Rose Santuci-Sofranko

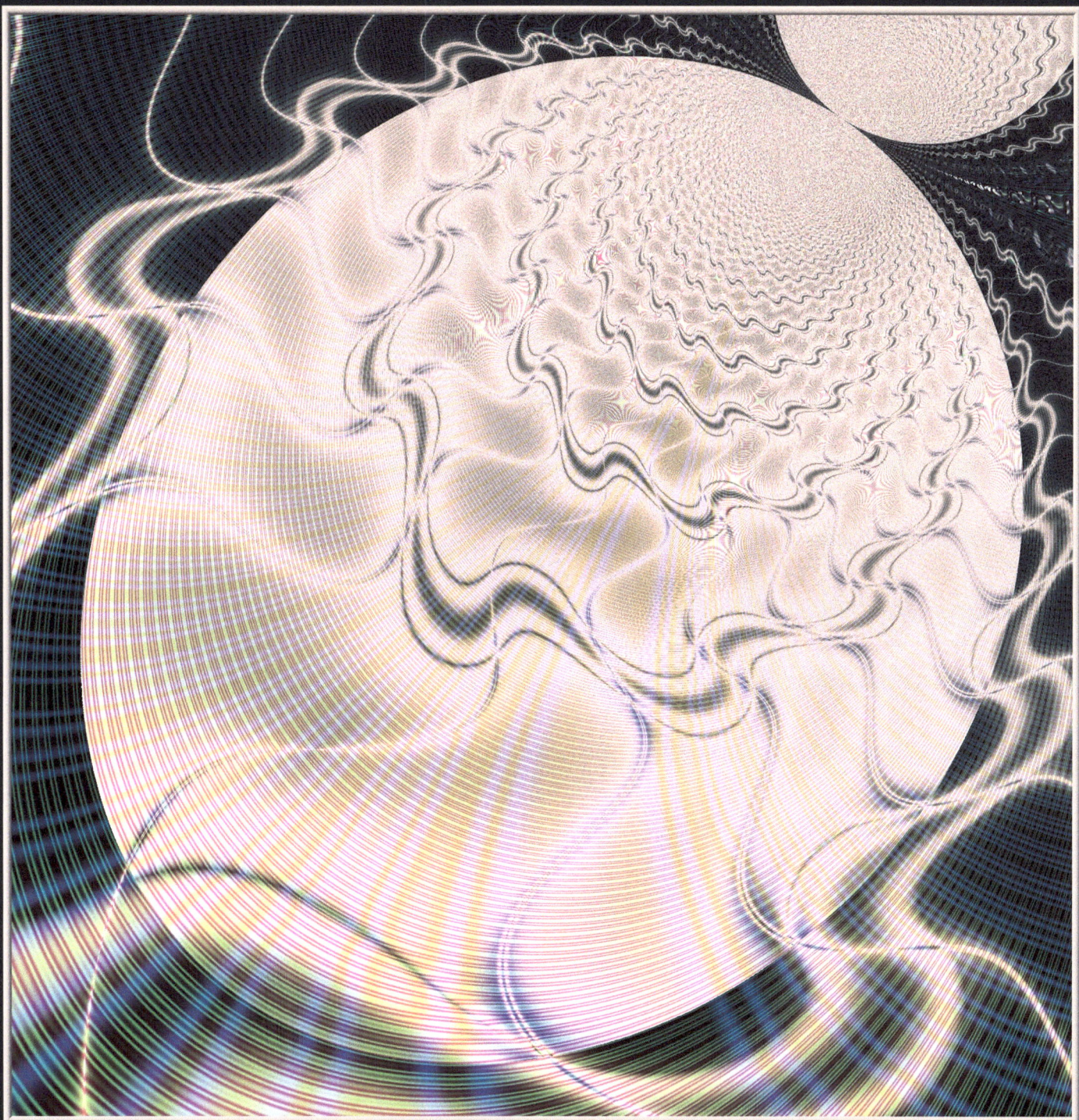

Rose Santuci-Sofranko

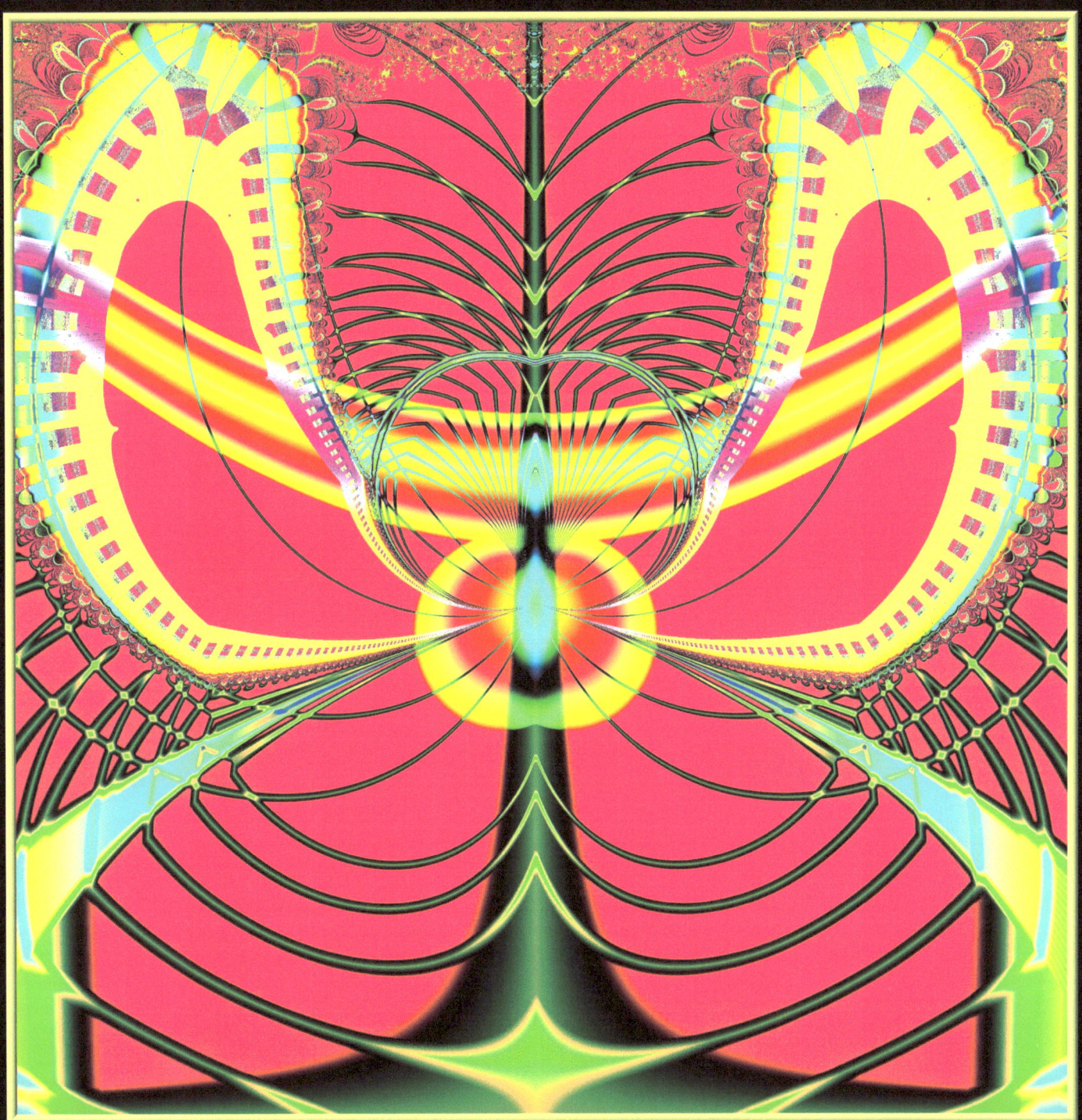

Rose Santuci-Sofranko

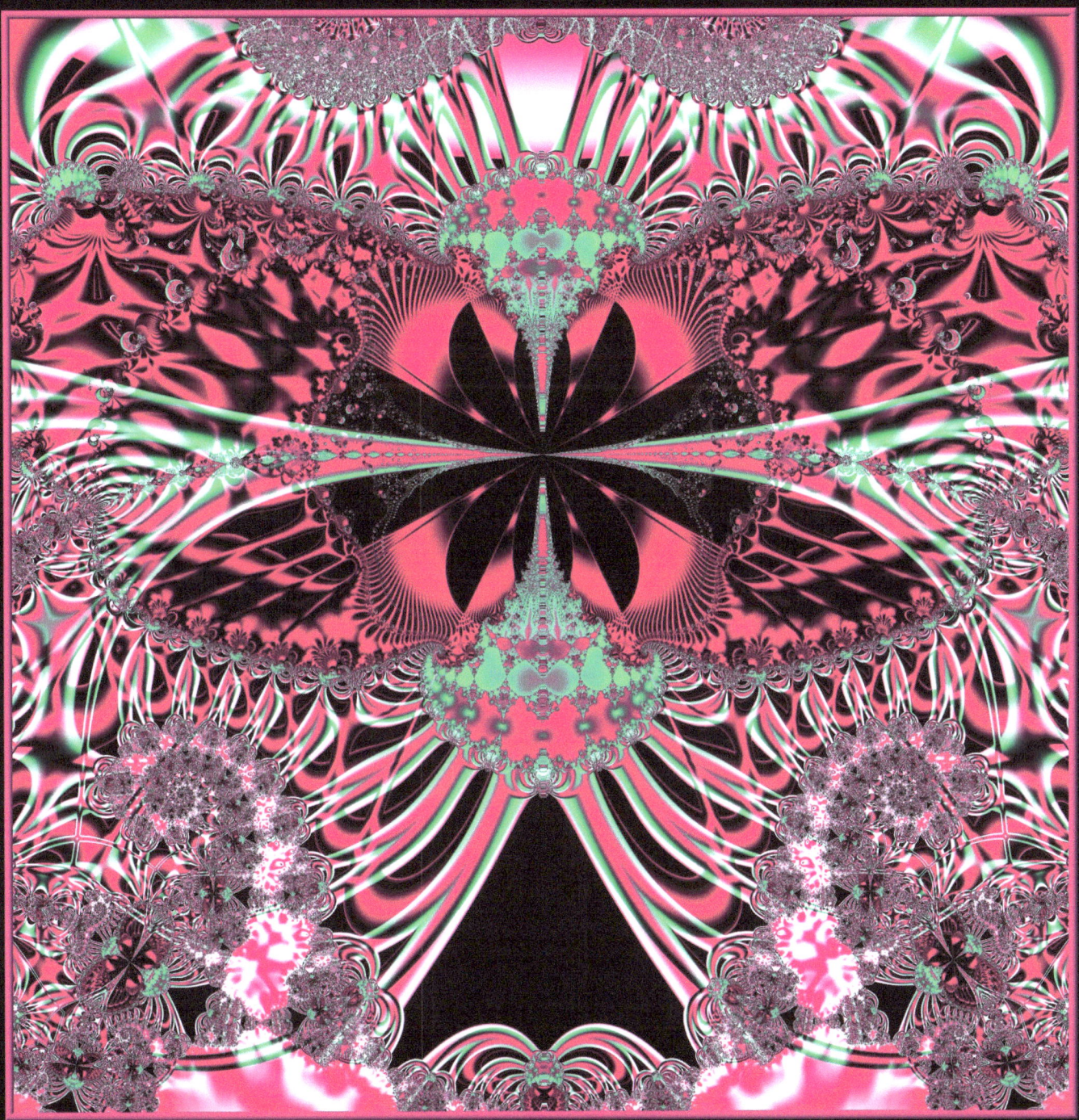

Rose Santuci-Sofranko

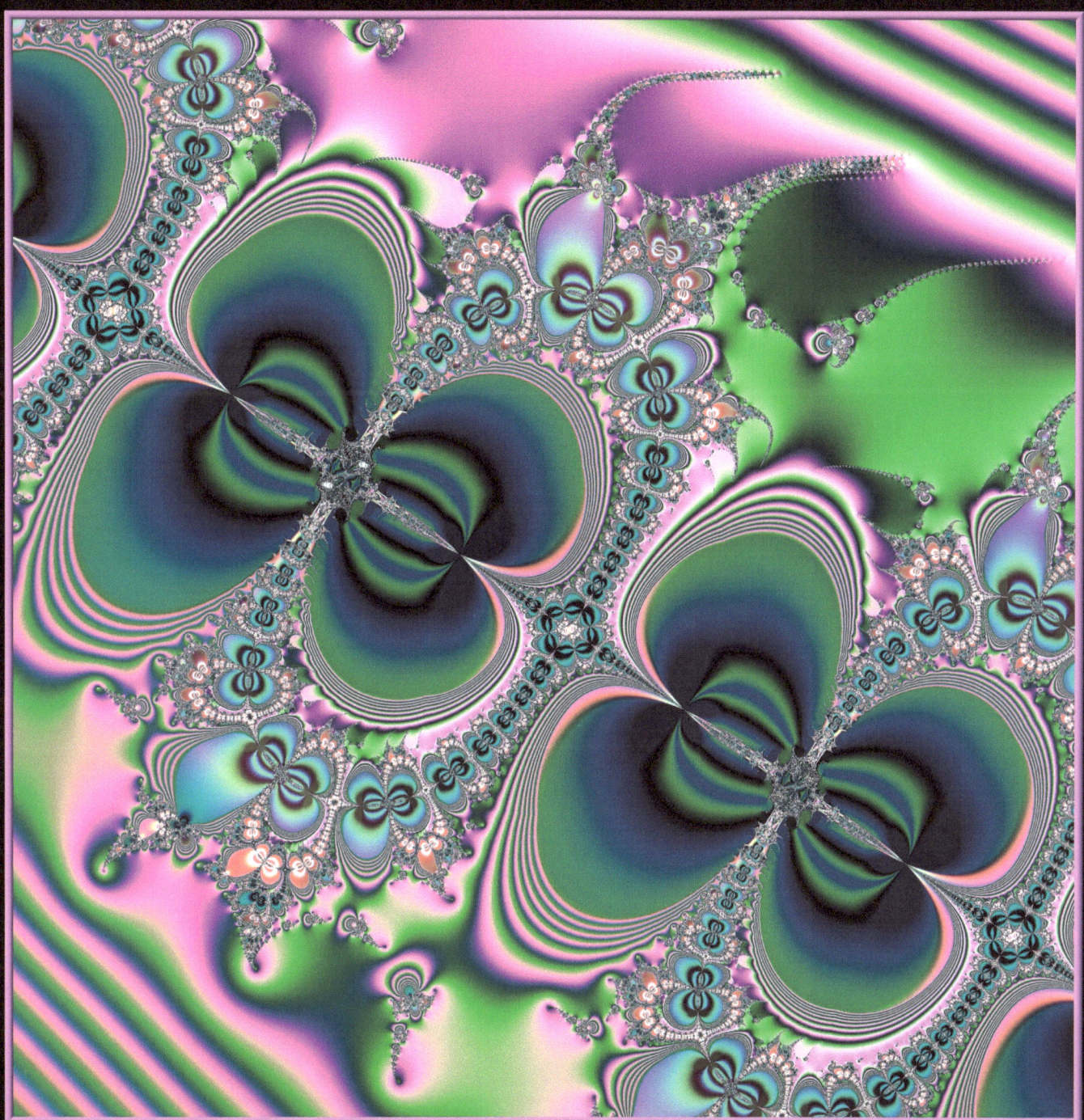

Rose Santuci-Sofranko

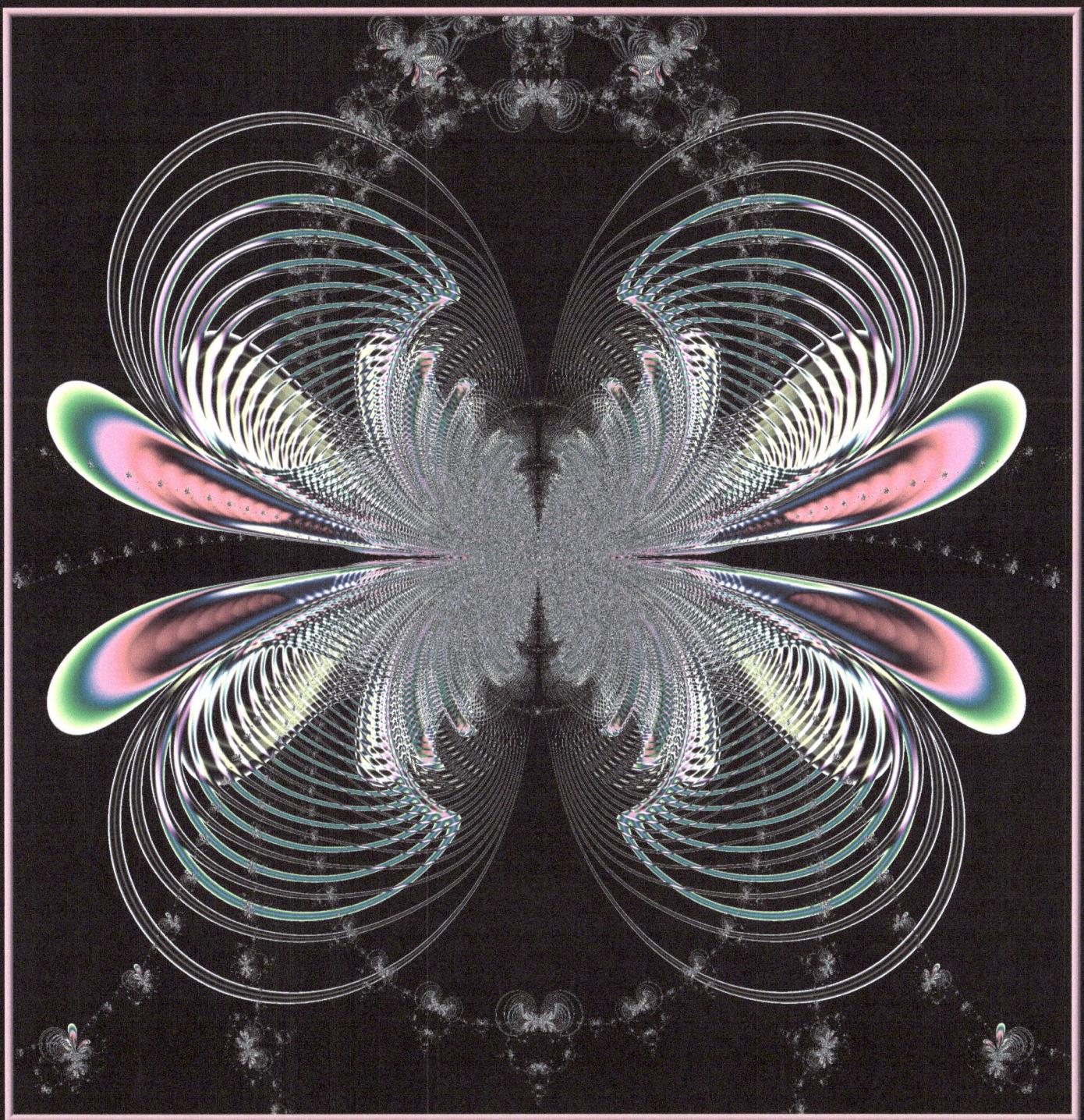
Rose Santuci-Sofranko

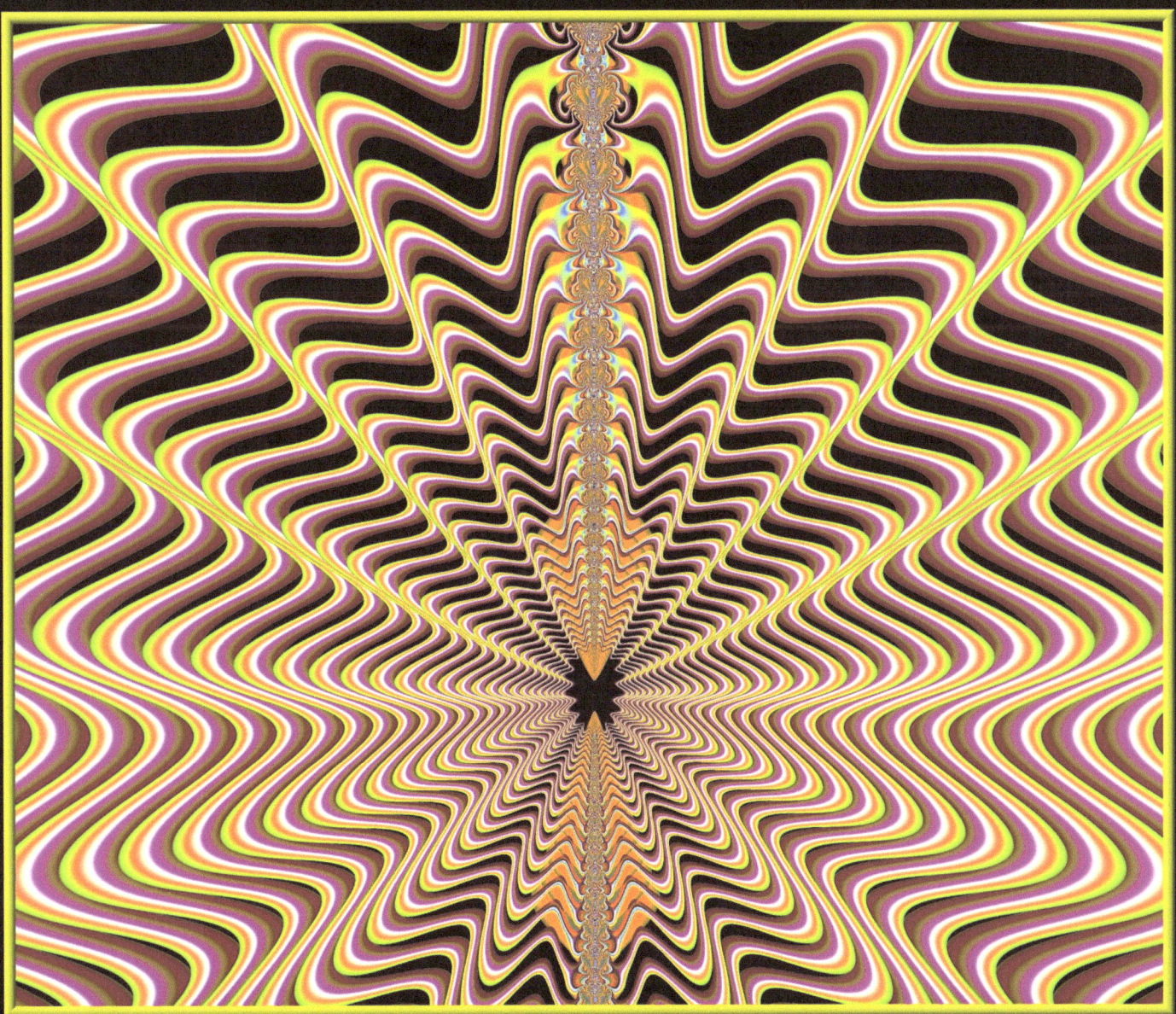
Rose Santuci-Sofranko

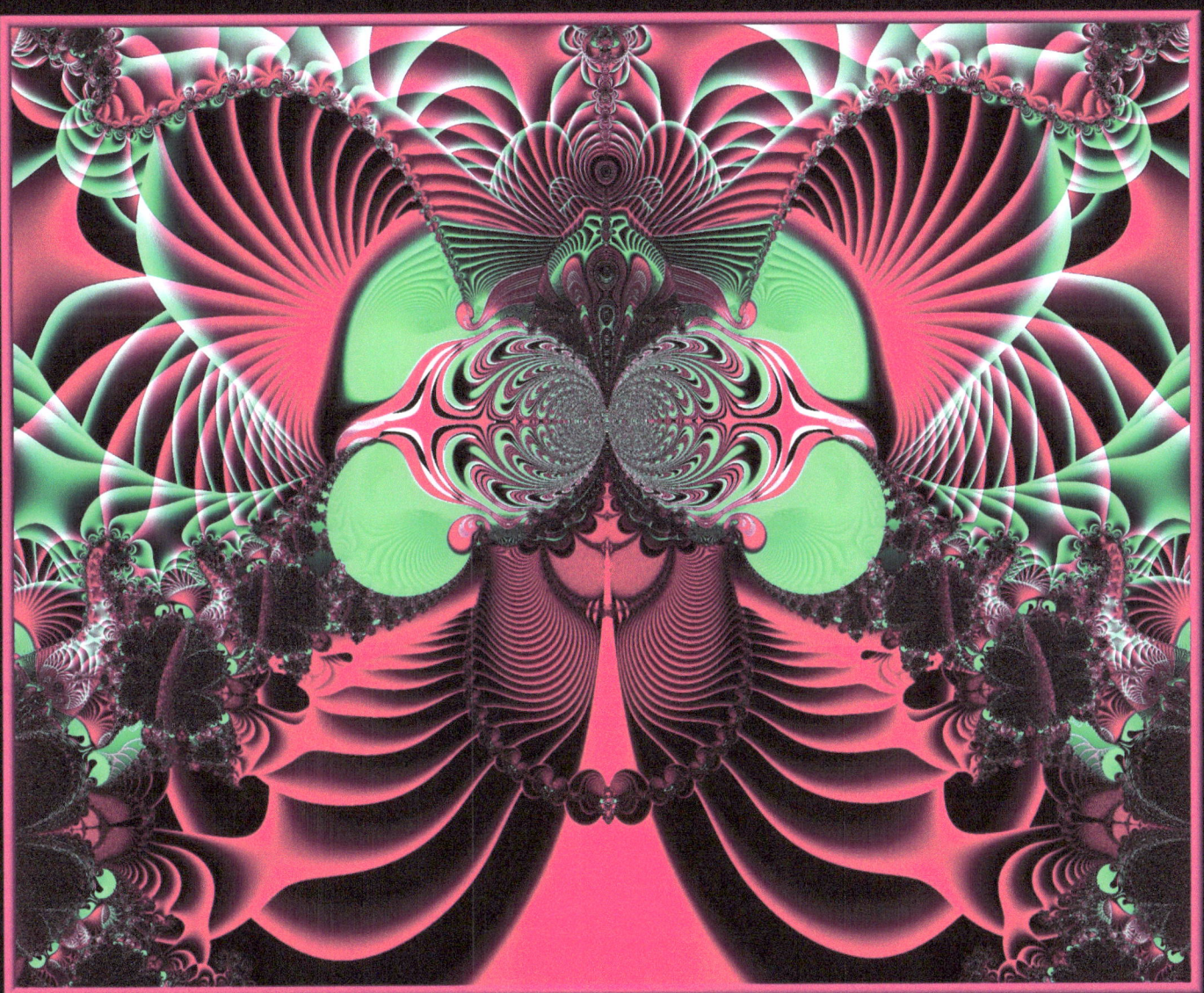
Rose Santuci-Sofranko

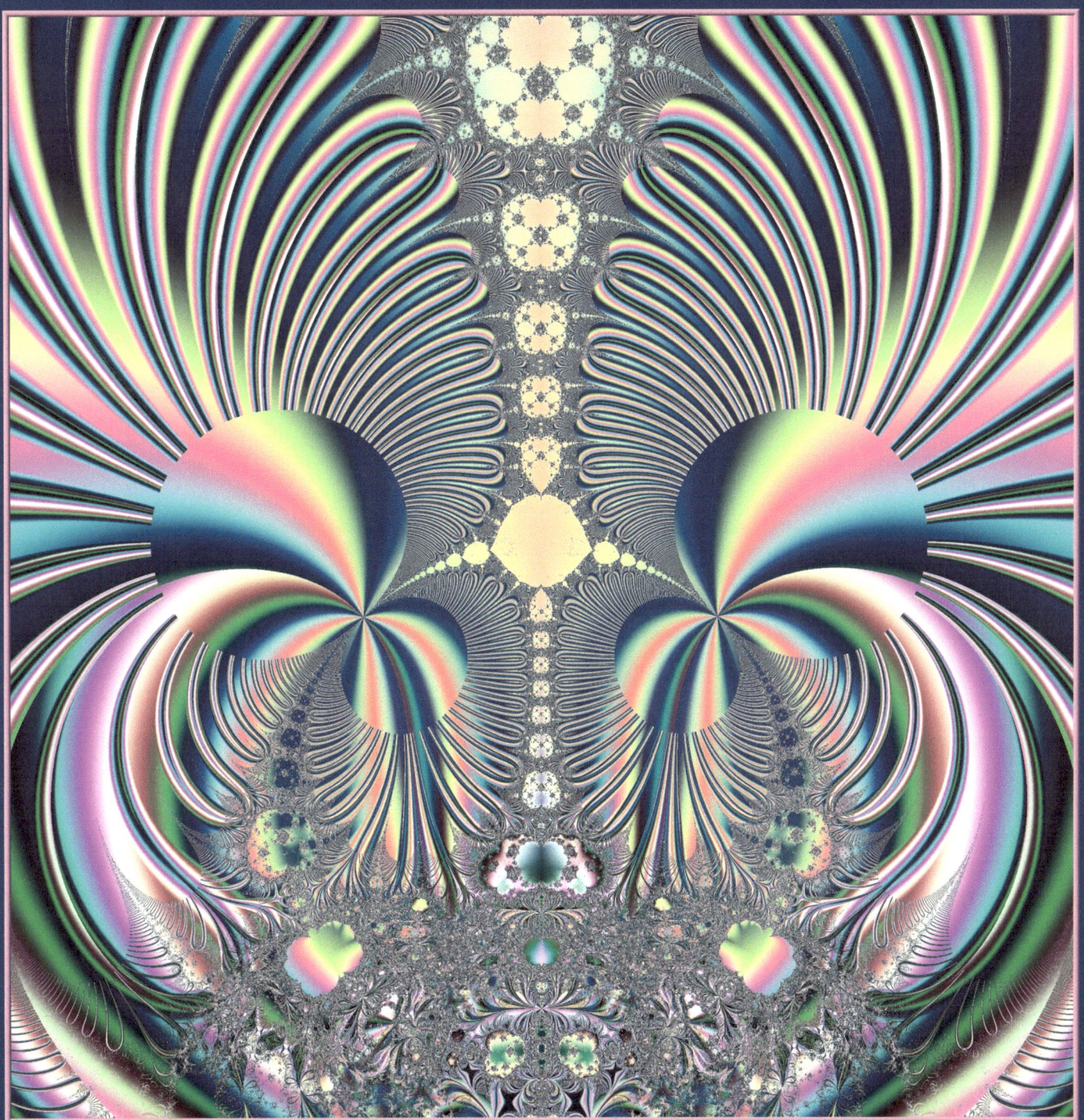

Rose Santuci-Sofranko

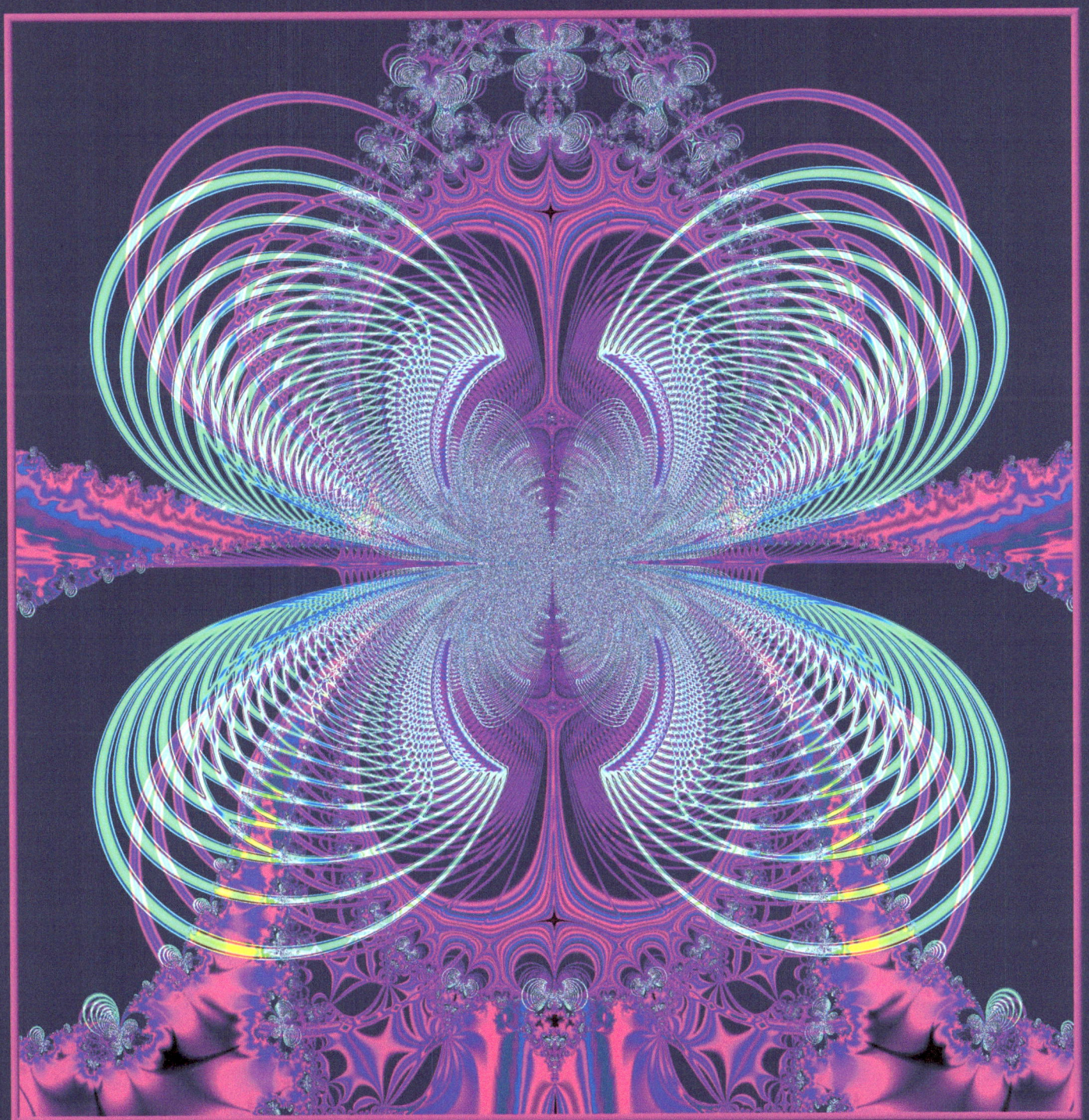
Rose Santuci-Sofranko

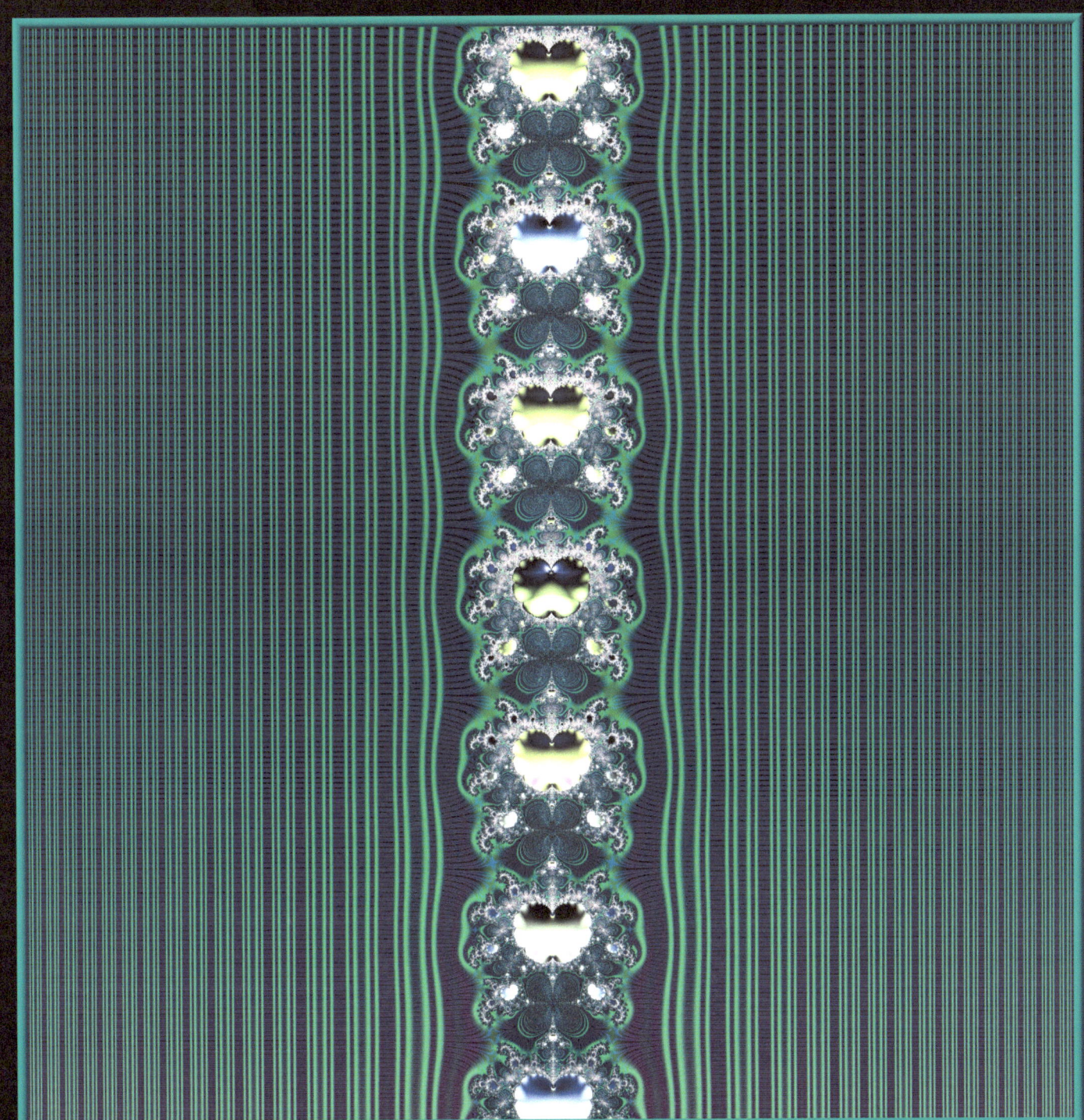

Rose Santuci-Sofranko

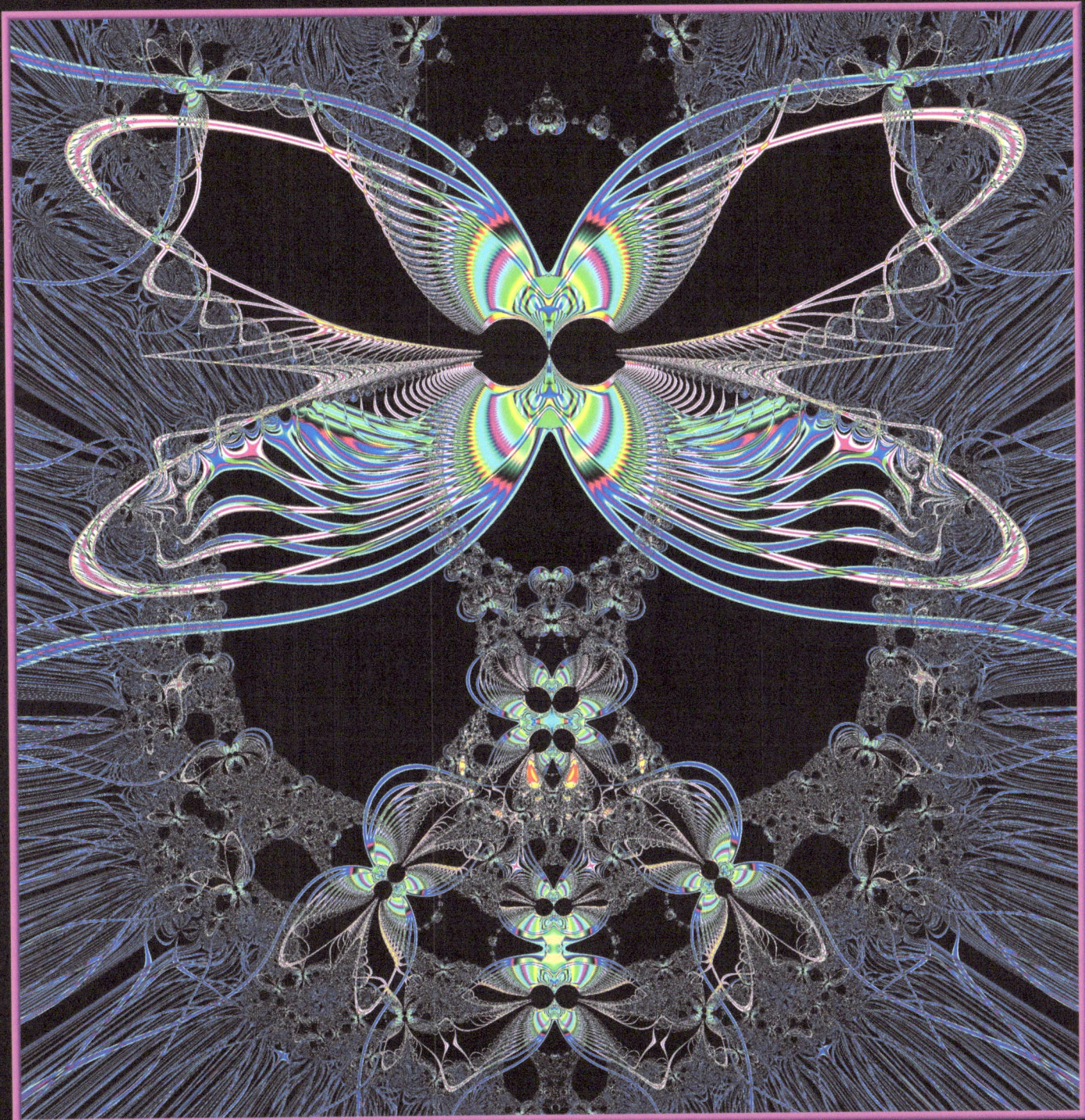

Rose Santuci-Sofranko

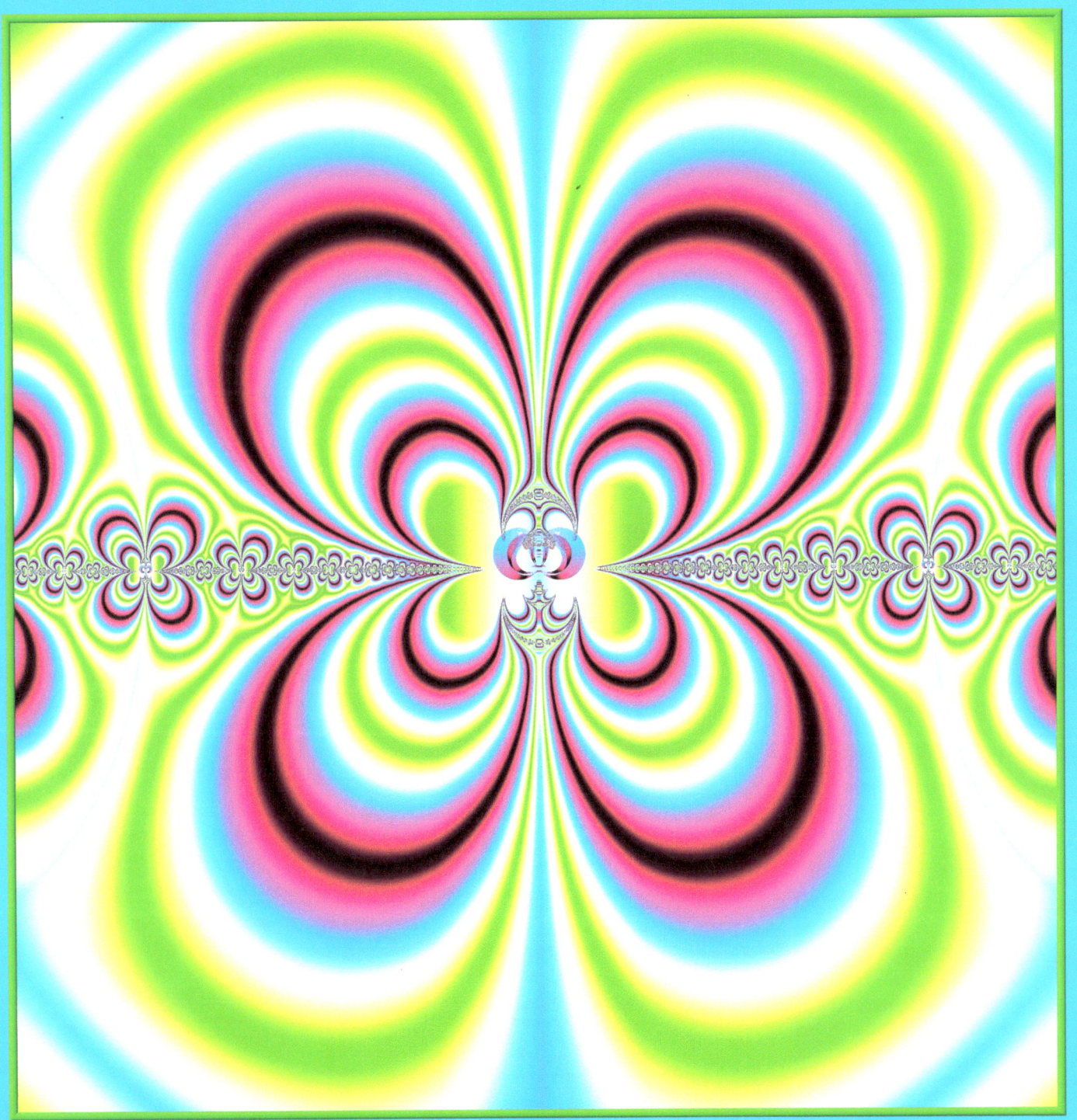

Rose Santuci-Sofranko

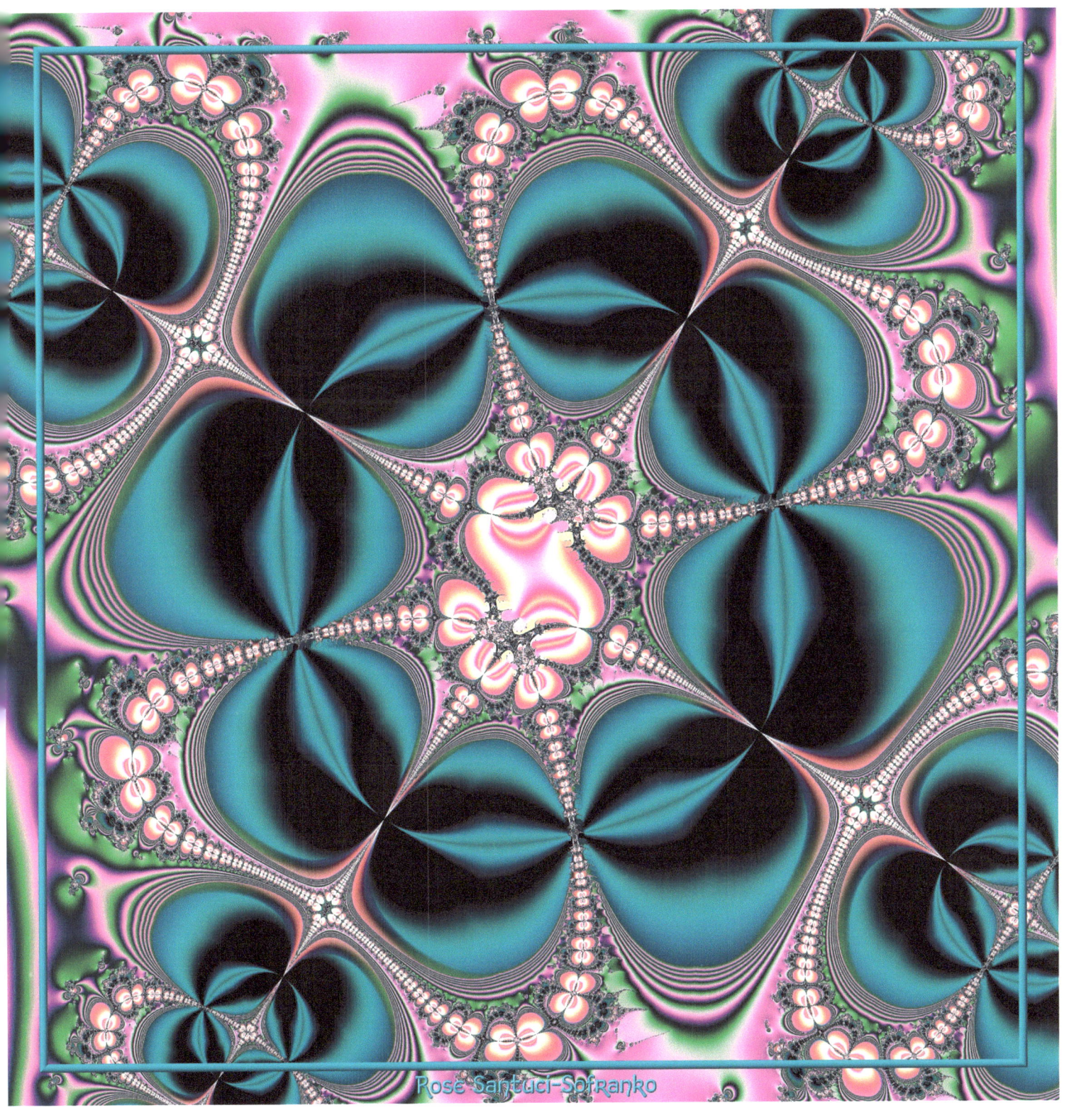
Rose Santuci-Sofranko

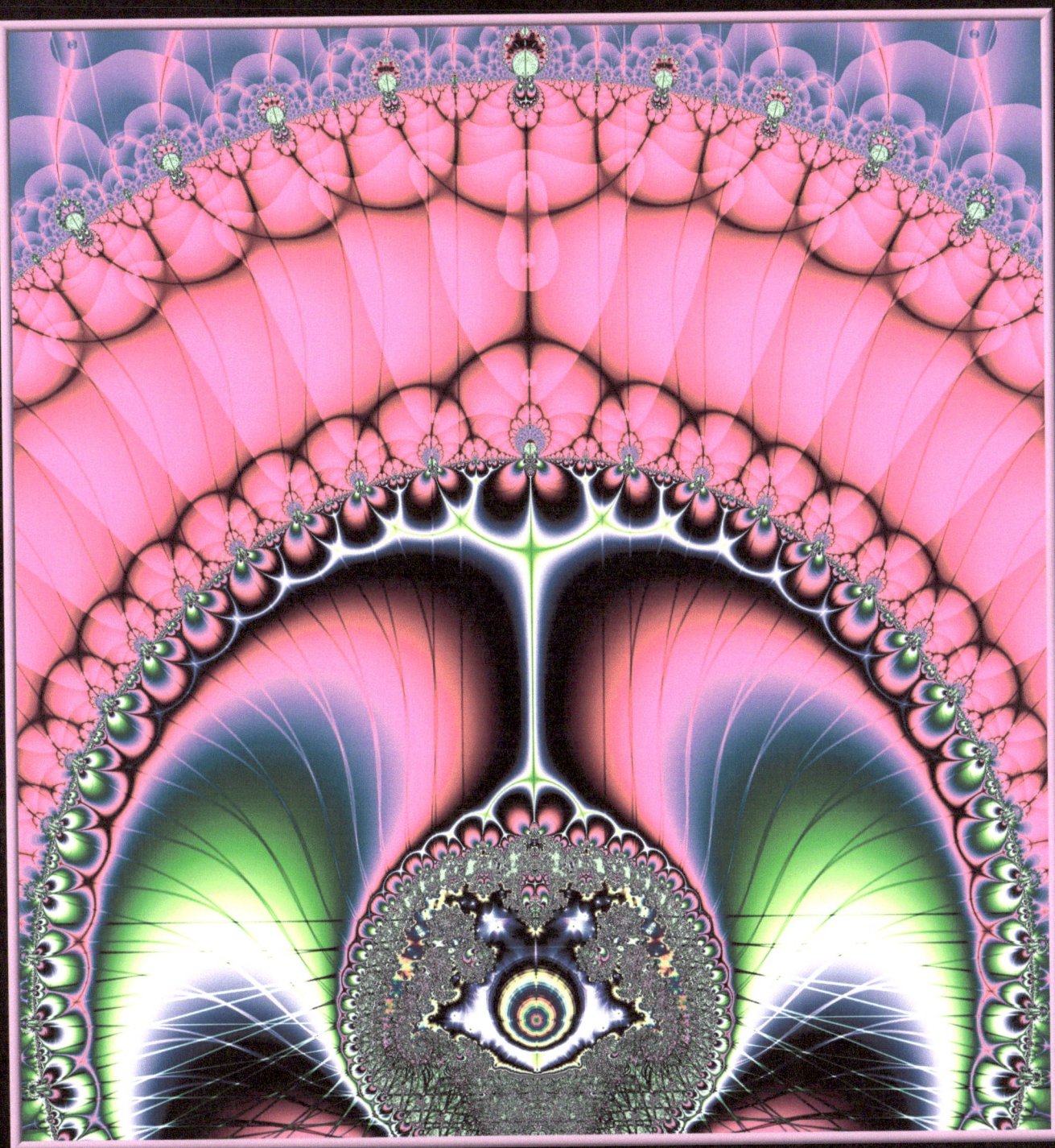

Rose Santuci-Sofranko

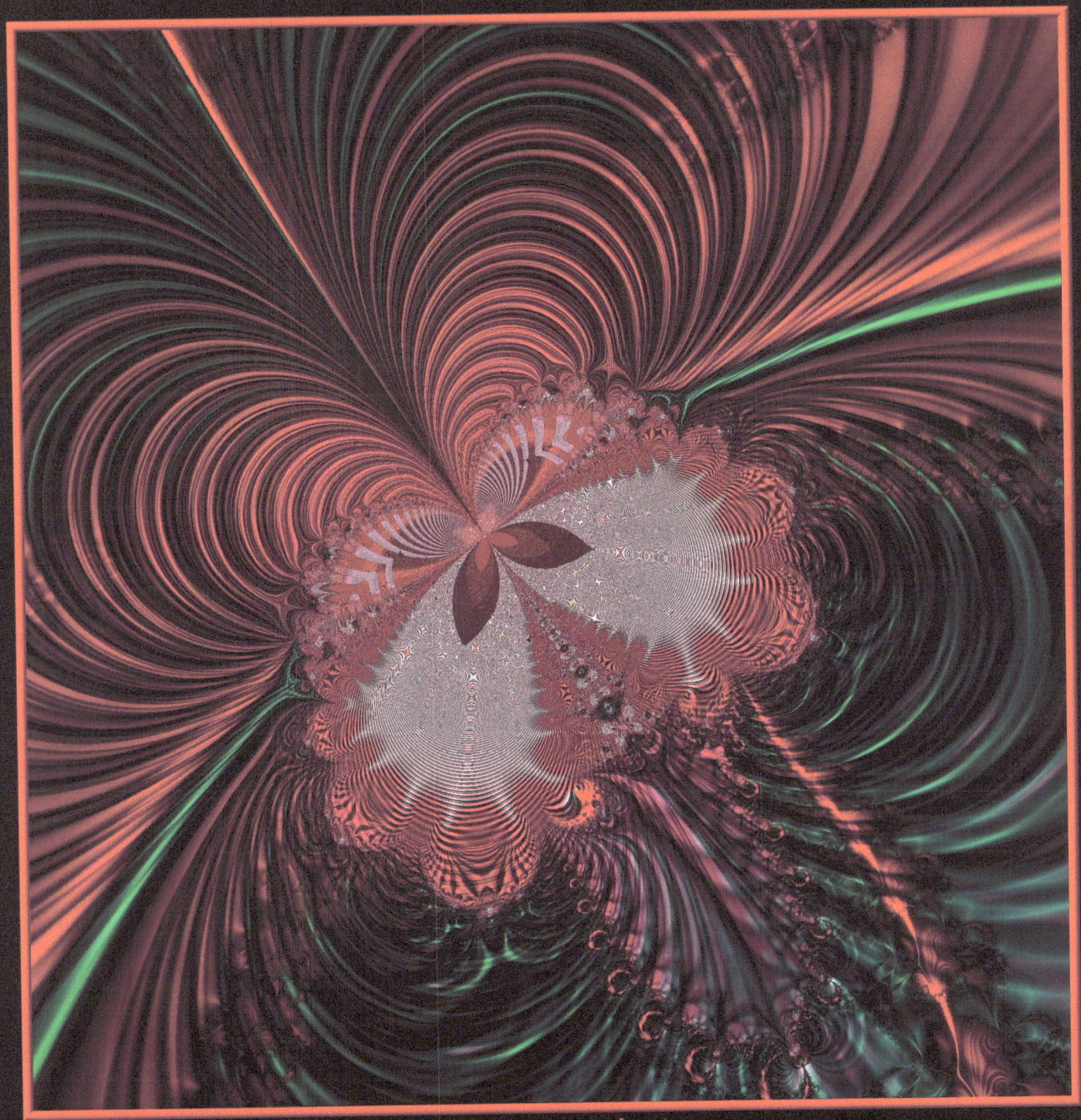
Rose Santuci-Sofranko

www.ingramcontent.com/pod-product-compliance
Lightning Source LLC
Chambersburg PA
CBHW051056180526
45172CB00002B/663